CHECKERBOARD BIOGRAPHY LIBRARY

U.S. PRESIDENTS

The
United States Presidents

WILLIAM H. HARRISON

ABDO Publishing Company

Heidi M.D. Elston

visit us at
www.abdopublishing.com

Published by ABDO Publishing Company, 8000 West 78th Street, Edina, Minnesota 55439.
Copyright © 2009 by Abdo Consulting Group, Inc. International copyrights reserved in all
countries. No part of this book may be reproduced in any form without written permission from the
publisher. The Checkerboard Library™ is a trademark and logo of ABDO Publishing Company.

Printed in the United States.

Cover Photo: Alamy
Interior Photos: Alamy p. 17; Corbis pp. 5, 9, 26; Getty Images pp. 14, 18, 23; iStockphoto p. 32;
    Library of Congress pp. 12, 16, 24, 27, 28, 29; North Wind pp. 10, 11, 15, 19, 25;
    Picture History pp. 13, 21

Editor: Megan M. Gunderson
Art Direction & Cover Design: Neil Klinepier
Interior Design: Jaime Martens

Library of Congress Cataloging-in-Publication Data

Elston, Heidi M.D., 1979-
  William H. Harrison / Heidi M.D. Elston.
     p. cm. -- (The United States presidents)
  Includes index.
  ISBN 978-1-60453-456-6
  1. Harrison, William Henry, 1773-1841--Juvenile literature. 2. Presidents--United States--
Biography--Juvenile literature. I. Title.

  E392.E45 2009
  973.5'8092--dc22
  [B]
                          2008027055

CONTENTS

WILLIAM H. HARRISON

William H. Harrison was the ninth president of the United States. He served as president for just one month. This is the shortest time spent in office by any U.S. president.

Before becoming president, Harrison served in the U.S. Army for 25 years. He rose in rank to major general. Harrison also worked in farming and tried his hand at business. After the **War of 1812**, Harrison entered politics. He served in both houses of Congress and in the Ohio state senate.

Harrison began his presidential term on March 4, 1841. At his **inauguration**, he caught a cold. He died one month later from **pneumonia**. Harrison was the first president to die in office.

As president, Harrison did not have time to accomplish great things. But as a military leader, Harrison played an important role in American history.

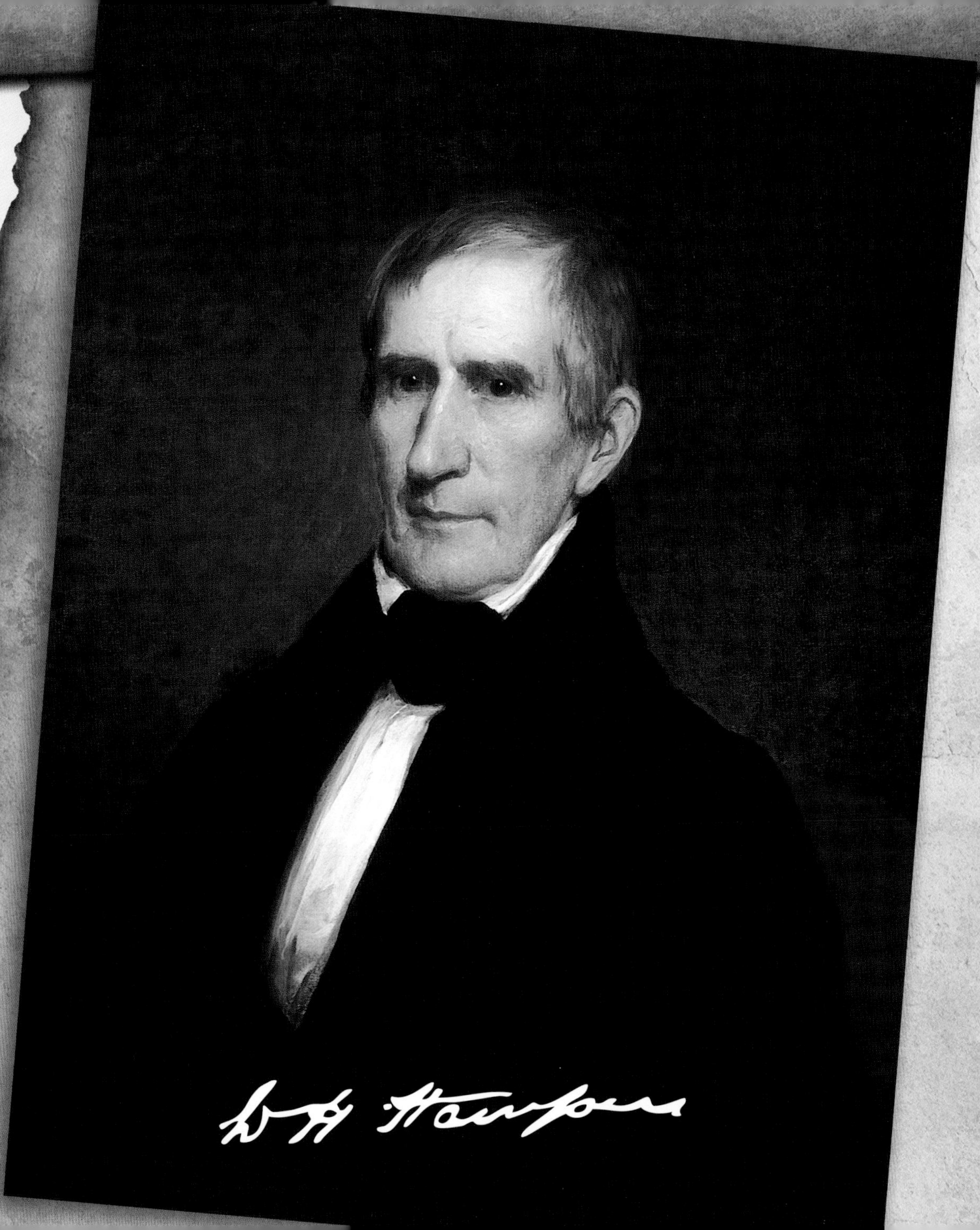

TIMELINE

1773 - On February 9, William Henry Harrison was born in Charles City County, Virginia.

1791 - Harrison joined the military as an ensign in the First Regiment of Infantry.

1794 - On August 20, Harrison fought at the Battle of Fallen Timbers.

1795 - Harrison married Anna Symmes.

1798 - Harrison resigned from the military; President John Adams appointed Harrison secretary of the Northwest Territory.

1800 - President Adams made Harrison governor of the Indiana Territory.

1811 - Harrison defeated Native Americans in the Battle of Tippecanoe.

1813 - Harrison fought victoriously in the Battle of the Thames.

1814 - Once again, Harrison resigned from the military.

1816 - Harrison won election to the U.S. House of Representatives.

1819 - Harrison was elected an Ohio state senator.

1825 - Harrison won election to the U.S. Senate.

1828 - President John Quincy Adams made Harrison minister to Colombia.

1836 - Harrison lost the election for president to Martin Van Buren.

1841 - On March 4, Harrison became the ninth U.S. president; William H. Harrison died on April 4.

DID YOU KNOW?

William H. Harrison was the last U.S. president to be born under British rule.

At 67, Harrison was the oldest man to be elected president in the 1800s.

Harrison was the first Whig president.

Harrison is the first president whose grandson later became president. His grandson Benjamin Harrison became the twenty-third U.S. president in 1889.

Harrison was the only president who studied to be a medical doctor.

Anna Harrison gave birth to the most children of any First Lady.

EARLY YEARS

William Henry Harrison was born on February 9, 1773, in Charles City County, Virginia. At the time, Virginia was a British colony.

William was the youngest of seven children. He had four sisters and two brothers. William's parents were Benjamin Harrison and Elizabeth Bassett Harrison. The Harrisons were wealthy and well known. They lived on a plantation named Berkeley on the James River.

Benjamin, William's father, was the governor of Virginia. He was called "the Signer." This is because he had signed the **Declaration of Independence**.

William studied at home until 1787. Then, he went to Hampden-Sydney College in Hampden-Sydney, Virginia. There, he studied classics and history.

FAST FACTS

BORN - February 9, 1773
WIFE - Anna Symmes
    (1775–1864)
CHILDREN - 10
POLITICAL PARTY - Whig
AGE AT INAUGURATION - 68
YEAR SERVED - 1841
VICE PRESIDENT - John Tyler
DIED - April 4, 1841, age 68

The Berkeley plantation, William's childhood home

In 1790, William decided to become a doctor. So, he left college and moved to Philadelphia, Pennsylvania. There, he studied medicine.

In 1791, Benjamin Harrison died. William was sad because he had been close to his father. By law, most of Benjamin's money and land went to his oldest sons. As the third son, William did not get as much money. Now, he had to get a job. So, he left his medical studies.

THE FRONTIER

On August 16, 1791, Harrison joined the military. President George Washington appointed him an **ensign** in the First Regiment of **Infantry**. Harrison was young, but he was determined. He gathered 80 men. Together, they headed into the western wilderness of the United States. There, they would fight Native Americans for land.

Harrison marched his men over the Allegheny Mountains to Fort Pitt in Pittsburgh, Pennsylvania. Then, they took boats down the Ohio River. They landed at Fort Washington in Cincinnati, Ohio. This area was called the Northwest Territory. It became home to Harrison for most of his life.

Harrison learned all he could about the military. He soon earned respect for his bravery. On August 20, 1794, Harrison fought at the Battle of Fallen Timbers. There, the U.S. Army defeated Native Americans.

Today, the site of the Battle of Fallen Timbers is a state park. It is located near Toledo, Ohio.

The Battle of Fallen Timbers ended fighting in the Northwest Territory. It also led to the Treaty of Greenville, which was signed on August 3, 1795. In it, Native Americans gave up claims to most of present-day Ohio. They also transferred parts of today's Michigan, Illinois, and Indiana to the United States. Afterward, Harrison rose to the rank of lieutenant. He then served as commander of Fort Washington.

The Miami Native Americans were living in parts of the Northwest Territory. Miami chief Little Turtle signed the Treaty of Greenville.

FAMILY AND CAREER

While at Fort Washington in 1795, Harrison met Anna Symmes. Anna had been born in New Jersey and was well educated. Harrison and Anna married that November.

Anna's father, Judge John C. Symmes, did not approve of the marriage at first. He felt Harrison's military career was too unstable to support a family. And, he knew his daughter would have to endure the hardships of frontier life. Yet Harrison eventually won over Judge Symmes.

Anna Harrison

The Harrisons had a long, happy marriage. They had six sons and four daughters. The family never had a lot of money. But they were close and loving.

The Harrison family home at North Bend

In 1797, Harrison became an army captain. He resigned the following year. Then, he and his family settled on a farm at North Bend, Ohio. They lived in a four-room log cabin. Over the years, Harrison added 12 more rooms to their home.

It cost a lot of money to feed the large Harrison family. Still, Harrison invited many friends, travelers, and politicians home for dinner. With the extra mouths to feed, they sometimes went through a whole ham in one day! The cost of feeding everyone used up most of Harrison's money.

President John Adams

Harrison enjoyed farming. But to support his family, he needed more money. In June 1798, President John Adams made him secretary of the Northwest Territory.

The following year, Harrison became the territory's first delegate to the U.S. Congress. In Congress, Harrison worked hard for Americans. People liked his ideas.

Harrison pushed Congress for the Land Act of 1800. This law changed the way land was sold. Before, land was sold in huge **tracts**. So, only rich people could afford it. The Land Act split land into smaller sections. It became easier for poor settlers to buy land.

Congress passed the Northwest Ordinance on July 13, 1787. This law provided for the government of the Northwest Territory. This region eventually became Ohio, Indiana, Illinois, Michigan, and Wisconsin. It also included part of Minnesota east of the Mississippi River.

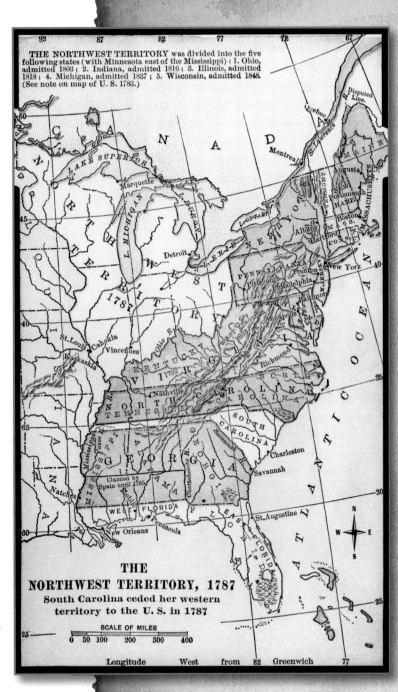

THE NORTHWEST TERRITORY was divided into the five following states (with Minnesota east of the Mississippi): 1. Ohio, admitted 1803; 2. Indiana, admitted 1816; 3. Illinois, admitted 1818; 4. Michigan, admitted 1837; 5. Wisconsin, admitted 1848. (See note on map of U. S. 1783.)

THE NORTHWEST TERRITORY, 1787
South Carolina ceded her western territory to the U. S. in 1787

SCALE OF MILES
0   50 100   200   300   400

Longitude   West   from   82   Greenwich   77

GOVERNOR HARRISON

In 1800, the Northwest Territory was divided into the Ohio and Indiana territories. President Adams named Harrison the first governor of the Indiana Territory. Harrison served as governor for 12 years.

Governor Harrison tried to improve the well-being of the local Native Americans. He barred alcohol sales to them. And, he ordered their **inoculation** against **smallpox**.

As governor, Harrison also made several treaties with Native American tribes. He gained many acres of their land in Indiana and Illinois for settlement.

Governor Harrison

16

While serving as governor of the Indiana Territory, Harrison and his family lived in present-day Vincennes, Indiana. Their home is called Grouseland and is open for tours.

Many Native Americans were upset about losing their land. So, they joined together under Shawnee Native American chief Tecumseh and his brother, known as the Prophet. In 1811, Harrison led American troops into battle. They defeated the Native Americans at Tippecanoe River near Lafayette, Indiana. The victory earned Harrison the nickname "Old Tippecanoe."

For a while, the Battle of Tippecanoe stopped problems between Native Americans and settlers. But by 1812, Native Americans were again attacking settlements.

President James Madison

Meanwhile, Harrison began fighting in the **War of 1812**. President James Madison made him a brigadier general. In 1813, Harrison was promoted to major general.

Later that year, Harrison recaptured Detroit from the British. Then on October 5, he won the Battle of the Thames. This battle

U.S. forces greatly outnumbered the British and Native American forces at the Battle of the Thames.

took place on the Thames River in Ontario, Canada. There, Harrison's troops defeated the British and their Native American **allies**. With this important victory, Harrison secured America's northwestern border.

WORKING FOR HIS COUNTRY

In 1814, Harrison once again quit the military. Then, he returned to his farm in North Bend. Besides farming, Harrison tried his luck in other businesses. But each failed.

Harrison still wanted to work for his country. He was popular in Ohio. So, many people encouraged him to run for Congress. In 1816, Harrison won election to the U.S. House of Representatives. He served as a representative until 1819. That year, Harrison was elected an Ohio state senator. He held this position until 1821.

Then in 1825, Harrison was elected to the U.S. Senate. He was a senator until 1828. That year, President John Quincy Adams made Harrison minister to Colombia. However, Andrew Jackson became president the next year. He sent a new minister to replace Harrison.

Harrison gained valuable political experience during his time as a representative, a state senator, and a U.S. senator.

BID FOR PRESIDENT

Many people thought Harrison could become president. He had a good record in the military and in Congress. So in 1836, the **Whig** Party nominated Harrison to run for president. However, the party was divided. So, it also nominated Daniel Webster and Hugh L. White. The **Democrats** nominated Martin Van Buren.

Harrison faced off against Webster, White, and Van Buren. Harrison's supporters believed he could unite the party. He did well in the election. But, he did not earn enough votes to win. Van Buren won the presidency with 170 Electoral College votes.

Shortly after President Van Buren began his term, the Panic of 1837 struck. The nation suffered an economic depression. Businesses closed, and many people lost their jobs. The nation suffered greatly. As a result, many Americans grew unhappy with President Van Buren. The depression affected his chances for reelection.

President Martin Van Buren

TIPPECANOE AND TYLER, TOO

The year 1840 brought another presidential election. Times were hard in the United States. Many people remained out of work.

The North and the South argued about slavery. Most people blamed the problems on President Van Buren.

Once again, the **Whig** Party nominated Harrison to run for president. Harrison chose John Tyler as his **running mate**. Tyler was a former senator from Virginia. The Whigs believed Tyler would help gain support in the South.

President Van Buren was Harrison's opponent. Harrison believed he could beat Van Buren in this election. He campaigned hard and gave many speeches.

Harrison's campaign was like a traveling carnival. He had floats in parades. He gave away hats and other things to gain voter support. Voters were reminded that Harrison was a military hero. His **slogan** "Tippecanoe and Tyler, Too!" was heard around the country.

A record number of people voted in the election. Harrison won the presidency! He received 234 electoral votes to Van Buren's 60. Tyler was named Harrison's vice president.

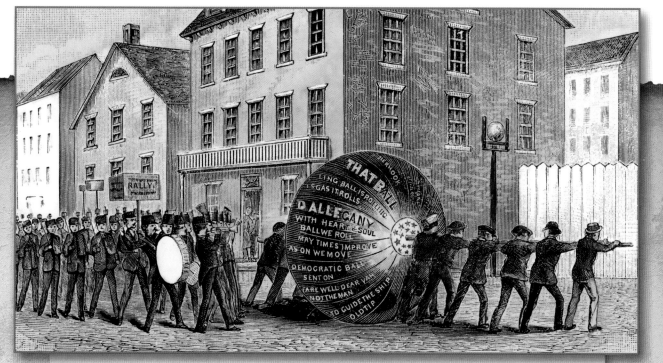

A group of Whig supporters pushed a ball covered in Harrison advertising for hundreds of miles. This started the common phrase, "Keep the ball rolling!"

THE NINTH PRESIDENT

In 1841, Harrison set out from Ohio for Washington, D.C. Mrs. Harrison was too sick to travel. So Jane Irwin Harrison, Harrison's daughter-in-law, went with him. She would act as White House hostess during Harrison's time in office.

On March 4, 1841, Harrison was **inaugurated** the ninth president of the United States. It was a windy, cold, and rainy day.

President Harrison's inauguration took place on the East Portico of the U.S. Capitol.

President Harrison gave one of the longest **inaugural** speeches ever. He stood in the cold without a hat or a coat.

President Harrison was worn out from his long campaign and caught a cold. Later that month, it developed into **pneumonia**. William H. Harrison died on April 4, 1841. It was a sad day for his wife, children, friends, and fellow Americans. Mrs. Harrison never made it to Washington, D.C. She was preparing to leave Ohio when she received the sad news that her husband had died.

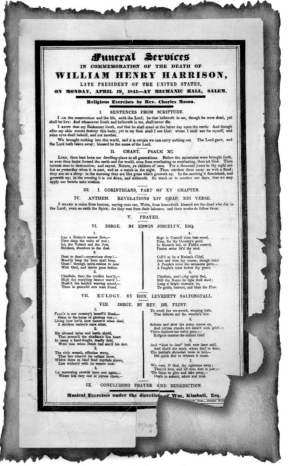

Harrison's funeral was held in Washington, D.C.

The U.S. government was in a tough position. At the time, the U.S. **Constitution** did not clearly say who should become president upon the death of the president. The United States had not been faced with this issue before. So, Vice President Tyler named himself president.

During his short time in office, President Harrison had named his **cabinet**. However, Tyler disagreed with Harrison's cabinet members on many issues. Tyler was a former **Democrat**. He still believed in many of the Democratic Party's ideas. President Tyler **vetoed** many **Whig**-supported bills. So, all the cabinet members except **Secretary of State** Daniel Webster quit.

Harrison served the shortest presidency in American history. People believe he could have been a great president. William H. Harrison remains one of the nation's respected military leaders.

John Tyler served the remainder of Harrison's term. He lost his bid for the presidency in 1844.

PRESIDENT HARRISON'S CABINET

MARCH 4, 1841– APRIL 4, 1841

- **STATE** – Daniel Webster
- **TREASURY** – Thomas Ewing
- **WAR** – John Bell
- **NAVY** – George Edmund Badger
- **ATTORNEY GENERAL** – John Jordan Crittenden

OFFICE OF THE PRESIDENT

BRANCHES OF GOVERNMENT

The U.S. government is divided into three branches. They are the executive, legislative, and judicial branches. This division is called a separation of powers. Each branch has some power over the others. This is called a system of checks and balances.

EXECUTIVE BRANCH

The executive branch enforces laws. It is made up of the president, the vice president, and the president's cabinet. The president represents the United States around the world. He or she oversees relations with other countries and signs treaties. The president signs bills into law and appoints officials and federal judges. He or she also leads the military and manages government workers.

LEGISLATIVE BRANCH

The legislative branch makes laws, maintains the military, and regulates trade. It also has the power to declare war. This branch consists of the Senate and the House of Representatives. Together, these two houses make up Congress. Each state has two senators. A state's population determines the number of representatives it has.

JUDICIAL BRANCH

The judicial branch interprets laws. It consists of district courts, courts of appeals, and the Supreme Court. District courts try cases. If a person disagrees with a trial's outcome, he or she may appeal. If the courts of appeals support the ruling, a person may appeal to the Supreme Court. The Supreme Court also makes sure that laws follow the U.S. Constitution.

QUALIFICATIONS FOR OFFICE

To be president, a person must meet three requirements. A candidate must be at least 35 years old and a natural-born U.S. citizen. He or she must also have lived in the United States for at least 14 years.

ELECTORAL COLLEGE

The U.S. presidential election is an indirect election. Voters from each state choose electors to represent them in the Electoral College. The number of electors from each state is based on population. Each elector has one electoral vote. Electors are pledged to cast their vote for the candidate who receives the highest number of popular votes in their state. A candidate must receive the majority of Electoral College votes to win.

TERM OF OFFICE

Each president may be elected to two four-year terms. Sometimes, a president may only be elected once. This happens if he or she served more than two years of the previous president's term.

The presidential election is held on the Tuesday after the first Monday in November. The president is sworn in on January 20 of the following year. At that time, he or she takes the oath of office:

I do solemnly swear (or affirm) that I will faithfully execute the office of President of the United States, and will to the best of my ability, preserve, protect and defend the Constitution of the United States.

Line of Succession

The Presidential Succession Act of 1947 defines who becomes president if the president cannot serve. The vice president is first in the line of succession. Next are the Speaker of the House and the President Pro Tempore of the Senate. If none of these individuals is able to serve, the office falls to the president's cabinet members. They would take office in the order in which each department was created:

Secretary of State

Secretary of the Treasury

Secretary of Defense

Attorney General

Secretary of the Interior

Secretary of Agriculture

Secretary of Commerce

Secretary of Labor

Secretary of Health and Human Services

Secretary of Housing and Urban Development

Secretary of Transportation

Secretary of Energy

Secretary of Education

Secretary of Veterans Affairs

Secretary of Homeland Security

BENEFITS

- While in office, the president receives a salary of $400,000 each year. He or she lives in the White House and has 24-hour Secret Service protection.

- The president may travel on a Boeing 747 jet called Air Force One. The airplane can accommodate 70 passengers. It has kitchens, a dining room, sleeping areas, and a conference room. It also has fully equipped offices with the latest communications systems. Air Force One can fly halfway around the world before needing to refuel. It can even refuel in flight!

- If the president wishes to travel by car, he or she uses Cadillac One. Cadillac One is a Cadillac Deville. It has been modified with heavy armor and communications systems. The president takes Cadillac One along when visiting other countries if secure transportation will be needed.

- The president also travels on a helicopter called Marine One. Like the presidential car, Marine One accompanies the president when traveling abroad if necessary.

- Sometimes, the president needs to get away and relax with family and friends. Camp David is the official presidential retreat. It is located in the cool, wooded mountains in Maryland. The U.S. Navy maintains the retreat, and the U.S. Marine Corps keeps it secure. The camp offers swimming, tennis, golf, and hiking.

- When the president leaves office, he or she receives Secret Service protection for ten more years. He or she also receives a yearly pension of $191,300 and funding for office space, supplies, and staff.

PRESIDENTS AND THEIR TERMS

PRESIDENT	PARTY	TOOK OFFICE	LEFT OFFICE	TERMS SERVED	VICE PRESIDENT
George Washington	None	April 30, 1789	March 4, 1797	Two	John Adams
John Adams	Federalist	March 4, 1797	March 4, 1801	One	Thomas Jefferson
Thomas Jefferson	Democratic-Republican	March 4, 1801	March 4, 1809	Two	Aaron Burr, George Clinton
James Madison	Democratic-Republican	March 4, 1809	March 4, 1817	Two	George Clinton, Elbridge Gerry
James Monroe	Democratic-Republican	March 4, 1817	March 4, 1825	Two	Daniel D. Tompkins
John Quincy Adams	Democratic-Republican	March 4, 1825	March 4, 1829	One	John C. Calhoun
Andrew Jackson	Democrat	March 4, 1829	March 4, 1837	Two	John C. Calhoun, Martin Van Buren
Martin Van Buren	Democrat	March 4, 1837	March 4, 1841	One	Richard M. Johnson
William H. Harrison	Whig	March 4, 1841	April 4, 1841	Died During First Term	John Tyler
John Tyler	Whig	April 6, 1841	March 4, 1845	Completed Harrison's Term	Office Vacant
James K. Polk	Democrat	March 4, 1845	March 4, 1849	One	George M. Dallas
Zachary Taylor	Whig	March 5, 1849	July 9, 1850	Died During First Term	Millard Fillmore

34

PRESIDENT	PARTY	TOOK OFFICE	LEFT OFFICE	TERMS SERVED	VICE PRESIDENT
Millard Fillmore	Whig	July 10, 1850	March 4, 1853	Completed Taylor's Term	Office Vacant
Franklin Pierce	Democrat	March 4, 1853	March 4, 1857	One	William R.D. King
James Buchanan	Democrat	March 4, 1857	March 4, 1861	One	John C. Breckinridge
Abraham Lincoln	Republican	March 4, 1861	April 15, 1865	Served One Term, Died During Second Term	Hannibal Hamlin, Andrew Johnson
Andrew Johnson	Democrat	April 15, 1865	March 4, 1869	Completed Lincoln's Second Term	Office Vacant
Ulysses S. Grant	Republican	March 4, 1869	March 4, 1877	Two	Schuyler Colfax, Henry Wilson
Rutherford B. Hayes	Republican	March 3, 1877	March 4, 1881	One	William A. Wheeler
James A. Garfield	Republican	March 4, 1881	September 19, 1881	Died During First Term	Chester Arthur
Chester Arthur	Republican	September 20, 1881	March 4, 1885	Completed Garfield's Term	Office Vacant
Grover Cleveland	Democrat	March 4, 1885	March 4, 1889	One	Thomas A. Hendricks
Benjamin Harrison	Republican	March 4, 1889	March 4, 1893	One	Levi P. Morton
Grover Cleveland	Democrat	March 4, 1893	March 4, 1897	One	Adlai E. Stevenson
William McKinley	Republican	March 4, 1897	September 14, 1901	Served One Term, Died During Second Term	Garret A. Hobart, Theodore Roosevelt

PRESIDENT	PARTY	TOOK OFFICE	LEFT OFFICE	TERMS SERVED	VICE PRESIDENT
Theodore Roosevelt	Republican	September 14, 1901	March 4, 1909	Completed McKinley's Second Term, Served One Term	Office Vacant, Charles Fairbanks
William Taft	Republican	March 4, 1909	March 4, 1913	One	James S. Sherman
Woodrow Wilson	Democrat	March 4, 1913	March 4, 1921	Two	Thomas R. Marshall
Warren G. Harding	Republican	March 4, 1921	August 2, 1923	Died During First Term	Calvin Coolidge
Calvin Coolidge	Republican	August 3, 1923	March 4, 1929	Completed Harding's Term, Served One Term	Office Vacant, Charles Dawes
Herbert Hoover	Republican	March 4, 1929	March 4, 1933	One	Charles Curtis
Franklin D. Roosevelt	Democrat	March 4, 1933	April 12, 1945	Served Three Terms, Died During Fourth Term	John Nance Garner, Henry A. Wallace, Harry S. Truman
Harry S. Truman	Democrat	April 12, 1945	January 20, 1953	Completed Roosevelt's Fourth Term, Served One Term	Office Vacant, Alben Barkley
Dwight D. Eisenhower	Republican	January 20, 1953	January 20, 1961	Two	Richard Nixon
John F. Kennedy	Democrat	January 20, 1961	November 22, 1963	Died During First Term	Lyndon B. Johnson
Lyndon B. Johnson	Democrat	November 22, 1963	January 20, 1969	Completed Kennedy's Term, Served One Term	Office Vacant, Hubert H. Humphrey
Richard Nixon	Republican	January 20, 1969	August 9, 1974	Completed First Term, Resigned During Second Term	Spiro T. Agnew, Gerald Ford

PRESIDENT	PARTY	TOOK OFFICE	LEFT OFFICE	TERMS SERVED	VICE PRESIDENT
Gerald Ford	Republican	August 9, 1974	January 20, 1977	Completed Nixon's Second Term	Nelson A. Rockefeller
Jimmy Carter	Democrat	January 20, 1977	January 20, 1981	One	Walter Mondale
Ronald Reagan	Republican	January 20, 1981	January 20, 1989	Two	George H.W. Bush
George H.W. Bush	Republican	January 20, 1989	January 20, 1993	One	Dan Quayle
Bill Clinton	Democrat	January 20, 1993	January 20, 2001	Two	Al Gore
George W. Bush	Republican	January 20, 2001	January 20, 2009	Two	Dick Cheney
Barack Obama	Democrat	January 20, 2009			Joe Biden

"Sound morals, religious liberty, and a just sense of religious responsibility are essentially connected with all true and lasting happiness." William H. Harrison

WRITE TO THE PRESIDENT

You may write to the president at:

The White House
1600 Pennsylvania Avenue NW
Washington, DC 20500

You may e-mail the president at:
comments@whitehouse.gov

GLOSSARY

ally - a person, a group, or a nation united with another for some special purpose.

cabinet - a group of advisers chosen by the president to lead government departments.

Constitution - the laws that govern the United States.

Declaration of Independence - an essay written at the Second Continental Congress in 1776, announcing the separation of the American colonies from England.

Democrat - a member of the Democratic political party. When William H. Harrison was president, Democrats supported farmers and landowners.

ensign (EHNT-suhn) - an infantry officer of what was formerly the lowest commissioned rank.

inaugurate (ih-NAW-gyuh-rayt) - to swear into a political office.

infantry - soldiers trained and organized to fight on foot.

inoculation - the process of giving a person or an animal a preparation made from killed or weakened germs or viruses to prevent disease.

pneumonia (nu-MOH-nyuh) - a disease that affects the lungs and may cause fever, coughing, or difficulty breathing.

running mate - a candidate running for a lower-rank position on an election ticket, especially the candidate for vice president.

secretary of state - a member of the president's cabinet who handles relations with other countries.

slogan - a word or a phrase used to express a position, a stand, or a goal.

smallpox - a contagious disease marked by a fever and blisters on the skin. The blisters often leave permanent scars shaped like little pits.

tract - an area of land.

veto - the right of one member of a decision-making group to stop an action by the group. In the U.S. government, the president can veto bills passed by Congress. But Congress can override the president's veto if two-thirds of its members vote to do so.

War of 1812 - from 1812 to 1814. A war fought between the United States and Great Britain over shipping rights and the capture of U.S. soldiers.

Whig - a member of a political party that was very strong in the early 1800s but ended in the 1850s. Whigs supported laws that helped business.

WEB SITES

To learn more about William H. Harrison, visit ABDO Publishing Company on the World Wide Web at **www.abdopublishing.com**. Web sites about William H. Harrison are featured on our Book Links page. These links are routinely monitored and updated to provide the most current information available.

INDEX